In thanks to God for my two beautiful girls, Brooke and Rosie.

Holiness.

CONTENTS

PREFACE

"Judge not, that you be not judged" (Matthew. 7:1).
These words from the mouth of Jesus have become a
huge part of the vocabulary of the Western world. The
prestigious title of the best known verse that belonged
to John 3:16, now belongs to Matthew 7:1. It's a good
verse, don't get me wrong, but the fact it has
dethroned John 3:16 lets us into the heart of the
current culture. "You can't judge the way I live" is the
cry of the day. This book, as the title makes clear, is
about holiness; why it's important, what it is, how we
grow in it, and what it looks like. Let me say straight
up that I am just as in need of a book on holiness as
the next person. I do not claim to have reached an
impressive level of holiness, quite the opposite. A lot
of what I talk about in the book are realities that I
have discovered because I have done the wrong thing,
and have learnt through mistakes.

5

The motivation for this book stems from a growing conviction that most Christians have an under-cooked understanding of what holiness is, especially the means God uses to achieve it in our lives. It's for this purpose that I have written this short book in the hopes that a greater understanding will lead to a greater holiness of life.

Holiness is stamped all over the Bible from beginning to end. It's even on the front cover – it's a holy book! We could even say that the contents are holy words. The words in the Bible are set apart from anything else that's ever been, or will be written. You cannot read the Bible without being drawn to that one word 'holy'. The God of the Bible is a holy God, and he calls us to be a holy people. However you view holiness, you cannot escape the fact that holiness is central to the Scriptures. Lots of authors have helped shape me, but I'm most thankful to the Puritans for giving me a clearer gospel-centred understanding of what it means to live the Christian life. S. D. G.

INTRODUCTION:

WHY SHOULD I CARE ABOUT HOLINESS?

Growing up I hated vegetables with a strange and fiery passion. Some of my least favourite childhood memories were the times when my parents would sit me down at the dinner table and then bring me a full plate of meat (yey!), and vegetables (Boo!). I don't know what it was about vegetables, but I just hated the sight of them, and I never wanted to give them the benefit of the doubt. They looked green, plain, healthy, and boring. Who wants to eat rabbit food, seriously? I couldn't even be tempted by the blatant lies of Pop-eye who promised me big and strong muscles. As I've gotten older, as with most people my taste buds have developed, and changed drastically. Vegetables aren't the revolting, bland, boring food items that they used to be. It turns out that vegetables are ok, even if I do prefer burgers, pizza, curry, and all things unhealthy. So what's this got to do with anything? My assumption is that this is how most of us view holiness. Sure it's healthy, and probably a good thing to desire, but it's kind of an optional extra that I can opt out on. Why stuff holiness down when I can concentrate on things that really matter, like hobbies and work?

You may wonder what the point is in talking about holiness in the first place? Isn't holiness for the Christian pastors and missionaries who are fired up for Jesus? Isn't it enough for me to just believe the gospel, attend church, and get on with life? I mean most of us want to live a better life and look more like Jesus, and we do desire to avoid the really terrible sins like sexual immortality, greed and power, but our lives seem to be quite alright without needing to think about holiness. Isn't it enough for me to just do what I'm doing, and plod along in the Christian life? Holiness kind of feels like the Biblical equivalent of eating up your vegetables.

We cannot and we must not avoid holiness. While growing in holiness sounds like the Biblical equivalent of eating up your greens, it should be the very opposite. There are plenty of reasons that Christians should care about holiness.

First, holiness is at the very heart of the Christian life because you were saved in order to be holy. That's one of the big reasons you believe in Jesus and are found in him. Holiness is one of the big reasons why God the Father chose you from before the foundation of the world. It's one of the big reasons God the Son came to earth to redeem you. It's one of the big reasons the Spirit was sent to dwell in you, and seal you with his power. There are many books in the Bible that show us this profound reality, but none so clear as the letter to the Ephesians. The Apostle Paul tells us that we are chosen by God the Father in eternity past, redeemed by God the Son in history, and given the gift of faith by God the Spirit in our lifetime, in order to be holy. Paul says this to us in the opening chapter of Ephesians;

Blessed be the God and Father of our Lord Jesus Christ who has blessed us with every spiritual blessing in the heavenly places, even as he chose us in him before the foundation of the world that we might be holy and blameless before him (Eph. 1:3-4).

The goal of our redemption is holiness. That's the great work that God is working in our lives from the first time that we put our trust in Jesus. J. I. Packer says that "in reality, holiness is the goal of our redemption. As Christ died in order that we may be justified, so we are justified in order that we may be sanctified and made holy". That's the first reason you should care about holiness – you were redeemed for the very purpose of it!

The second reason you should care about holiness is because holiness puts the gospel on display, and draws sinners to Jesus Christ. I'm not sure who actually said, "Preach the gospel, and if necessary use words", but we all know that the saying is rubbish. The gospel is first and foremost a declaration of what God has done to save fallen humanity. Faith comes by *hearing* the word, and hearing the word of Christ (Rom. 10:17). If anyone tries to tell you that you don't need to share the message of the cross to preach the gospel they are just plain wrong. God is a God who works through his word, and it is the word that makes us born again to a living hope (1 Pet. 1:23). A gospel without words is absolutely pointless, and cannot save anyone. But a gospel that isn't accompanied by works is often powerless as well. Of course God *can* work through our words even when our lives are living in contradiction to it, and he often does with me! But that's not what we should be aiming for because a gospel life that goes with the gospel message is a powerful tool in evangelism. When a life that's filled with gospel-shaped living shares the message of the cross, people get saved and God is glorified. I witnessed this while I was living on the Sunshine Coast in Australia. The church service had finished and we all left the vicinity to head down to the beach at night to order takeaway and hang out. The next thing we know a man from India walks up to us and begins asking who we are. A few of us began sharing the gospel with him. These were the words of my friend who eventually became a Christian, "I have never seen Ganesh, or Krishna, or any Hindu god change anyone the way I have seen Jesus Christ change you lot." Sadly, I haven't witnessed many stories like this, but this was a really wonderful thing to be a part of. Just after preaching the message of the beatitudes on the sermon on the mount Jesus says, "Let your light shine before others so that they may see your good works and give glory to your Father who is in heaven" (Matt. 5:16). This is why holiness matters to Jesus, and why holiness should matter to us. Non-believers are watching us whether we like it or not. We declare a message of gospel transformation, and so the world watches on to see if what we say is true. When people see the gospel at work in our lives they will give glory to our Father in heaven. What a great motivation to care about, and desire holiness!

The third reason we need to care about holiness is because holiness brings with it a sense of peace and confidence in who we are in Christ. The Bible gives us three identity markers to assure us that we are Christians and on the way to glory; that we believe in the Lord Jesus Christ, that we love and obey the Lord Jesus Christ, and that we love and serve one another. In other words, you know you are a Christian if you believe in Jesus, obey his commands, and love his people. Holiness is one of the signs that we are truly born again and not deceived with a false profession of faith. Paul says, "to set your mind on the things of the flesh is death, but to set your mind on the things of the Spirit is peace and life." Notice peace is one of the consequences of living by the Spirit. There is no peace for us when we are living according to the flesh. Some of the lowest moments of my life have been the times of living in intentional sin. It strangles my joy, takes away my peace, and ruins my relationship with God. Of course I don't lose my salvation in those moments, but I certainly lose the enjoyment of my salvation.

The fourth reason you should care about holiness is because that's what we will be in the world to come. A lot of people in this world want heaven, without realising that it's the opposite of the things they want here on earth. It makes no sense to long for heaven and not long for holiness. Holiness is glory begun, as glory is holiness consummated. J. C. Ryle said that, "Heaven is a holy place. The Lord of heaven is a holy Being. The angels are holy creatures. Holiness is written on everything in heaven. The book of Revelation says expressly that nothing defiled will enter heaven (Rev. 21:27)... How shall we ever be at home and happy in heaven if we die unholy... what possible enjoyment would you find in heaven? The saints pleasures are not your pleasures, their tastes are not your tastes, their character is not your character. How could you possibly be happy if you had not been holy on earth?" Ryle is saying that heaven will be a very unhappy place for someone who cares nothing for holiness. Holiness is what is in store for everyone who puts their faith and trust in Jesus. When we die and be with the Lord, we will be perfectly holy.

HERE'S WHY THIS MATTERS

Holiness isn't an optional extra for the Christian, but a necessity. The Scriptures teach that Christ has already broken the power of sin. He does not pay the penalty for our sin to then leave us in its power (Rom. 6:14). A person born again with a new nature will produce the fruits of that new nature. Now we know that we will continue to struggle against sin. We're liars if we pretend that we don't sin (1 Jn. 1:8), and we will only be perfectly sinless when Christ returns (1 Jn. 3:2). I am not advocating for the heresy of Christian perfectionism. To side with Christian perfectionists is to have a too low view of sin, and a too high view of self. However, the Christian will be marked with a new and transformed life. While we won't be sinless, we will sin less. This is the work that God is producing in us by his Spirit. God does not create new people and leave them unchanged any more than someone can be hit by a truck and stay the same. Without holiness we will not see the LORD (Heb. 12:14). The people rejected by Jesus on judgement day will be those who have lived lives of lawlessness (Matt. 7:21-23). The Scriptures affirm over and over that progressive holiness is essential for salvation. Not because holiness is the root of our salvation, but because it is the fruit. A new and transformed life will produce good works. We need to get this order super clear in our minds. You were saved in order to be holy, not the other way around. The Scriptures affirm from Genesis to Revelation that salvation comes by the grace of God alone, through faith alone, in Christ alone (Gal. 2:16). We are not saved *by* holiness, but *for* holiness. If you try and make yourself right with God by being holy you will only fail and stand condemned. Anyone who seeks to be justified by the law has fallen from grace and is severed from Christ (Gal. 5:4). We are only righteous in the sight of God because he has given to us an alien righteousness, the righteousness of Jesus Christ, who lived the perfect life we should have lived, and died the death we deserved to die. Now risen, he calls his people into a new life of holiness!

REFLECTION QUESTIONS

- Have you found holiness to be a boring topic in the past?
- Why is holiness extremely important in the Christian life?
- What are some of the ways that God works through the holiness of his people?
- What is the connection between the gospel and holiness?

CHAPTER ONE
THE BIBLE AND HOLINESS

Before I became a Christian I was obsessed with the gym scene. I had competed in bodybuilding competitions in Australia and had won hundreds of trophies – I lie… I won zero. I would have seriously liked to have won trophies. While I didn't win any trophies I was living for them and working out every day for the chance of one day sticking a half-naked man trophy on my cabinet. Lovely right? I worked hard, lifted big, ate big, and trained like my life depended on it. Looking back, my genetics were pretty rubbish, and so I was never going to win anything. There was always someone bigger and better than me, and he had the drugs to do what I wasn't willing to do! You would be surprised by how much my identity as a bodybuilder shaped my life. Everything about my life was centred around the gym and working out. Every relationship I had suffered because I was all about myself, the gym, my body, and the gains. My bodybuilding identity would shape the way I walked, ate, spoke, acted, and thought of myself. But it's not surprising is it? When we have an identity that matters to us we allow that identity to shape who we are. And the same is true of the Christian life. Who we are in Christ needs to lead to how we are to live. This took me a really long time to figure out because I assumed that you just take a "be holy" verse out of context and try to live it out. It wasn't until I realised the grand sweep of the Biblical story that I realised that was both an un-Biblical approach, and impossible anyway. You can't just 'be holy' by pulling yourself up by your bootstraps. How we live is always grounded in who we are. This is especially true of the Christian life.

It won't surprise you to know that the Bible has a lot to say about holiness. The word 'holy' appears so many times that you wouldn't be able to count it.

19

When most of us think about holiness we naturally think of specific things we need to do. Holiness is following the Ten Commandments, obeying the Bible, and following Jesus. While the Bible can sometimes emphasize holiness in this way it primarily uses the word 'holiness' in a positional sense. What do I mean by that? Well, 'holy' is a status that God has declared us to be. He has already made us holy through Jesus Christ. Therefore we need to think about this aspect of holiness before thinking about how we are to grow up into it. You are already holy!

GOD THE HOLY ONE

The Bible regularly identifies God as the Holy One of Israel (Isa. 40:25; Ez. 39:7; Ho. 11:9; Jer. 50:29). There are many great scholars who have gone into great detail about what the holiness of God is. While holiness can mean purity in an outward sort of way, it primarily means *being set apart*. God being holy means that he is distinct and set apart from everything else. This makes sense when you think about it because God is God, and we are not. Everything that has come into being has come into being through God, and so only God is God, everything else is creation. That is the big distinction between God and everything else – He is Creator, everything else is created. God is completely *other* than his creation in that he alone is all wise, simple, spirit, infinite, eternal, unchanging, independent, all powerful, all knowing, all present, with pure justice, righteousness, goodness and mercy. There is a sense in which God's holiness also means purity, as Charnock says, "God possesses a perfect and unpolluted freedom from all evil." The Bible emphasises the holiness of God throughout; Holy, holy, holy is the LORD of hosts, the whole earth is full of his glory (Isa. 6:3), Holy, holy, holy, is the Lord God Almighty, who was and is and is to come (Rev. 4:8), Who is like you O LORD, among the gods? Who is like you, majestic in holiness, awesome in glorious deeds, doing wonders? (Ex. 15:11). God's holiness, unlike ours derives from himself as Edward Leigh says, "God's holiness is that

21

excellency of his nature, by which he gives himself unto himself, doing all for himself, and in all, and by all, and above all, aiming at his own pleasure and glory; or it is the absolute purity of his nature and his abhorring of evil."

MADE HOLY BY THE HOLY GOD

God is completely holy and he cannot stand in the presence of sin without consuming the sinner. Therefore, when God delivered us from our sin in Christ he simultaneously set us apart as his own possession. The Christian has been made holy by the holy God. This is a definitive action on God's part, it is something that has been done to us already in the past tense. Now this might strike you as a bit strange especially if you have been told that holiness is something that we need to grow in. How can I say that holiness is something that we already are? Well, let me prove it to you. There are plenty of passages in the Bible that help us here, so we'll look at a few.

We'll begin with the book of Leviticus. Leviticus answers the question, "How can a holy God dwell with an unholy people?" It's been the problem throughout the first few books of the Bible. God has redeemed his people, but they are stiff-necked, unholy, and they have hearts that keep going astray. How is it possible for a holy God to dwell with a sinful people like that? Rather than being a boring book that we skip past, Leviticus is a vitally important book that we need to read and digest – don't skip it in your yearly reading plan! In Leviticus we find a God who has made a way for his people to dwell in his midst through the sacrificial system. Aaron the priest was called upon to offer sacrifices on behalf of the people of Israel for the forgiveness of sins. The overall picture can sometimes be lost on us, but notice the ordering in the book, because it's vital. God is the one who *makes* Israel holy by the sacrificial system. The people of Israel are made holy through the means that he has provided (Lev. 1-16). Holiness is something that the people of God *are*. It's only after the opening sixteen chapters that God then tells the people of Israel to be who they are (Lev. 17-27). The people of Israel have been made holy through the sacrificial system, and then they are called to become what they are – that is holy.

The next passage I want us to look at is from Paul's first letter to the Corinthians. This is a great letter to get stuck into. However many times you've read it, it doesn't take long to realise that these guys are super messed up! This is one messed up church. I read it thinking, "These are the least holy people that I've ever seen in my life. Look at how little they have grown in holiness!" And so when you read the opening verses of the letter, you can't help but feel flabbergasted. Paul begins the letter by calling the Corinthians, "The holy ones", and "The sanctified in Christ Jesus" (1 Cor. 1:1-2). Has Paul lost his marbles? Does he even know who these guys are and what they get up to? They're a complete mess! How on earth can Paul call them "the holy ones in Christ?"

Paul was able to call the Corinthians holy because holiness/sanctification is a position before it is something we do. Sanctified was a status that God declared the Corinthians to be in Jesus. It can't possibly be referring to their character and conduct because Paul spends the entire letter rebuking them for their behaviour. Paul, instead is referring to their status and what God has *already* done to them in Christ. Sanctified is who they are.

BE WHO YOU ARE

The Corinthian church have been called the sanctified in Christ. Yet notice how Paul uses their position in Christ as the means to urge them on in holiness. Paul begins his letter by calling them holy, and then urges them to press on and live that holy life. Paul does this all throughout the letter, but one clear example of this comes in the sixth chapter;

Do you not know that the unrighteous will not inherit the kingdom of God? Do not be deceived, neither the sexually immoral, nor idolaters, nor adulterers... will inherit the kingdom of God. And such were some of you. But you were washed, sanctified and justified in the name of the Lord Jesus Christ and by the Spirit of our God.

Paul's exhortation to be more holy in conduct is to point the church to the fact that they are already holy through Jesus Christ and by the Spirit. I wonder if you have friends who quote the above passage out of context by leaving the last sentence out of it? In the past, I have hit Christians over the head to be more holy without grounding it in the reality of their position in Christ. Maybe that's the way you have always understood it. But Paul isn't talking about immorality and licentiousness in order to guilt trip the church in Corinth. He's trying to show them that an unholy life is completely out of step with who they are. That's why he says, "And such *were* some of you." It's not who you are anymore because you have been cleansed in the name of Jesus Christ. It wouldn't make sense for a bodybuilder to walk around humbly, ignoring his body, and shoving down muffins. It makes sense to be an egotistical maniac when your whole life is spent at the gym looking in the mirror. It doesn't make sense to be humble. In the same way it doesn't make sense for someone washed and sanctified by Christ to go on living in the sin that once enslaved them. That's just not you anymore. The Christian who has been washed, justified, and sanctified by Christ has a whole new nature, and no longer has the old heart of stone that they used to have. The Christian no longer needs to live in sin because Christ has broken the power of sin. To go and live in the sin that once enslaved us makes no sense because for freedom Christ has set us free (Gal 5:1).

And you might be thinking that this is a one off that I have found during my devotional times. Can it really be the case that the impetus to holiness is always in light of what God has done for us? Well, before you begin to think this is a one off, know that this is the same approach Paul takes in Ephesians 4:17-24; Colossians 3:1-10 and various other places. This is a pattern that is all over the Bible. The writers of the New Testament never tell us to live a certain way just for the sake of it. How the Christian is to live is always grounded in who the Christian is. Now that you're aware of it you'll see it everywhere! In fact, it may even change the way you read the Bible, because it certainly did that for me. Our active holiness comes out of who we have been made to be in Jesus - the reality that God has already made us holy through Christ and by the Spirit. Holy is who God is. Holy is who he has made you to be. And so Christian, be holy, for God is holy.

REFLECTION QUESTIONS

- What does it mean that God is holy?
- How is God's holiness different to the holiness that we have?
- Is holiness something that we are, or something that we need to be?
- Can you think of any other passages that would suggest that holiness is first something that has definitively happened to you?
- Can you think of any commands to us that are *not* driven by what God has already done for us in Christ?

CHAPTER TWO

UNION AND HOLINESS

The best day of my life was the day the chapel doors swung open and my bride walked through. I will never forget that moment, no matter how much I was staring at a blurry white-dressed woman because of my watery eyes. From that day on God did something absolutely incredible, he made two people into one. The Bible speaks of marriage as a union between a husband and a bride. God takes the singular man, and the singular woman, and he makes them one flesh – it's marvellous! The vows between a husband and a wife make this clear when they say, "I take you… to be my wedded wife, to have and to hold, from this day forward, for better, for worse, for richer, for poorer, in sickness and in health, to love and to cherish. Till death do us part, according to God's holy ordinance; and thereto I pledge myself to you." I gave myself and everything I own to my wife when God joined us together. My wife gave herself and everything she owns to me when God joined us together. There is a profound oneness about our relationship that cannot be undone. That's why divorce is such a tragedy, it splits asunder that which should stay together. But marriage isn't an end in and of itself, it is pointing to something far more spectacular.

The Bible says that marriage points to the great mystery of Christ and the church. The church has been wedded to Christ like a bride to her husband. It is, as Paul describes it, a profound mystery. The church has a real mystical union with the Lord Jesus Christ. Union with Christ is the very heart of the gospel. You might be surprised to know that justification isn't the primary way that the New Testament speaks about salvation. You might be even more surprised to learn that it's neither redemption or adoption. Union with Christ is the primary way that the Bible speaks about salvation. The term appears one hundred and sixty four times in the New Testament. The Bible speaks of our being 'in Christ', and 'Christ in us'. It also speaks in terms of a marriage relationship with Jesus. John's gospel speaks of Christ being the vine and we the branches. The Epistles talk about the church being the body and Christ the head. In other words, Christ himself is our life. Every person was born dead in Adam, because Adam was our representative head, the one we are 'in'. Every Christian is born again in Jesus, and now Jesus reigns as our representative head because we have been brought 'into' him by the Spirit. This is one of the big distinctions between our union with Christ and our union with Adam. We are united to Adam through biological reproduction. Union with Christ is not a natural process, but a work of the Spirit when he brings us the new birth and gives us faith. The Spirit connects the believer to Jesus Christ who is the one in whom is life. The Christian only has eternal life when he is in the one who is the life. This means that salvation is much better than God giving you a ticket to heaven. I think a lot of our evangelistic work makes it appear that Jesus is the ticket that God gives you so you can finally get into heaven. The gospel isn't that you get a ticket to heaven, the gospel is that you get Jesus himself. Jesus is our saviour who holds himself out to us and gives us all that he is. In other words, on the wedding day, when a Christian trusts in Christ, Jesus says, "All that I am I give to you." Martin Luther put it like this, "Who can ever begin to appreciate this royal marriage? Who can comprehend the riches of this glorious grace? Christ, the rich divine groom marries this poor, wicked whore, redeems her from all her evil, and adorns her with all his goodness. It's now impossible for her sins to destroy her, for they are laid on Christ and swallowed up in him. She has her righteousness in Christ which she can claim as her very own. And in the face of death and hell she can say "If I have sinned, nevertheless, the one in whom I trust, my Christ has not sinned. All that is his is mine. And all that is mine is his". This is what the Reformers called, 'The great exchange'. Christ has taken my sin and filth, and in exchange has given me his perfect righteousness because I am united to Christ by faith. If Jesus stands from a distance and gives us the blessings of justification, sanctification, and glorification, then we are lost. Jesus is the justified one (1 Tim. 3:16). If we are not connected to Jesus, the righteous one, we will never be saved. John Calvin said, "As long as Christ remains outside of us, and we are separated from him, all that he has suffered and done for the salvation of the human race remains useless and of no value to us. Therefore, to share in what he has received from the Father he had to become ours and to dwell within us." I hope you're beginning to see what I'm saying here, that salvation is ultimately being in Christ and receiving all of the blessings 'in him'.

BRANCHES ATTACHED TO THE VINE

What does this have to do with our topic on holiness? It sounds a little out of context to be talking about this doesn't it? Far from being irrelevant, union with Christ has everything to do with holiness because without being united to Christ we can't be holy! Just as we cannot receive justification without being united to Christ, so we cannot receive sanctification (holiness) without being united to Christ. That's because Christ is the one who is sanctified/set apart (Jn. 17:19). What does it mean that Jesus, the already holy one, sanctified himself? Thomas Torrance said, "The holiness of the church is derived from God through Jesus Christ… he sanctified himself in the human nature that he took from us, that we might be sanctified." You might be wondering if it's Biblical to say that we receive our sanctification by being in Jesus, because isn't he the one who sanctifies us by the Spirit? The best place for us to look is a passage in 1 Corinthians 1:30 where Paul says, "and because of him you are in Christ Jesus, who became to us wisdom from God, righteousness and *sanctification* and redemption." So rather than saying that Jesus sanctifies us, Paul is saying that Jesus is our sanctification. Likewise, Jesus teaches his disciples this reality when he says that they are only sanctified when they are united to him, "I am the true vine and my Father is the vinedresser… Abide in me and I in you. As the branch cannot bear fruit by itself, unless it abides in the vine, neither can you unless you abide in me. I am the vine, you are the branches. Whoever abides in me and I in him, he it is that bears much fruit for apart from me you can do nothing." (Jn. 15:1, 4-5). The Christian can only bear fruit when he is united to Christ. If we are not united to Christ we are unable to bear fruit, because apart from being in Jesus we can do nothing. We are completely dependent on our union with Christ in order to be holy. Sanctification then, just like justification, glorification, and adoption comes to us through our union with the risen Lord Jesus Christ. Any attempt to try and explain holiness without union will fail because it's a foundational aspect of what it means to be holy.

Let us think for a moment about one of the big implications to what I am saying. A believer is only justified, sanctified and glorified when they are connected to the risen Lord Jesus Christ by faith, through the Spirit. There is an inseparable link between who Jesus is and the blessings that Jesus gives us. This ultimately means that you can't have a Christian who is justified and not sanctified. There have been waves of people who have tried to advocate for the idea that you can be justified without growing in sanctification. We've seen that this is impossible. If salvation is about receiving Christ himself, then how can someone be attached to Jesus and not be receiving sanctification? I believe this is one of the dangers we face when we split the person of Christ from the blessings of the gospel. If sanctification is not about being united to Christ by faith then it can be something we don't need to worry about. As long as Jesus stands back and gives me the gift of justification, I don't need to worry about anything else. But as we've seen this is not a Biblical way of talking about salvation, because we only have the blessings of the gospel through union. And that means that every single person united to Christ will be sanctified, and be in the process of sanctification. We are sanctified because we are in Jesus Christ.

REFLECTION QUESTIONS

- Were you surprised to learn that union with Christ was so central in the Bible?
- Why do you think that union with Christ has gone by the by in evangelicalism?
- How does Paul's picture of marriage help you to understand union with Christ?
- How does union with Christ make sanctification necessary in the Christian life?

CHAPTER THREE

GROWING IN HOLINESS

Growth was an important term for me in my gym days. Everything about my life centred around that word 'growth'. I wanted my arms to grow, my chest to grow, my legs to grow, my back to grow, and my shoulders to grow. If anything wasn't growing I was pretty miserable, though I soon worked out why it was. You don't grow as a bodybuilder if you don't put the right food into your body. If I go to the gym and train hard, only to come home and eat Haribo and doughnuts I'm in trouble. You need to get good meat into your stomach or you are not going to get any bigger. Getting the right food into your body is essential for growing your body. And the same is true in the Christian life. You will not grow as a Christian if you don't eat the right food. You need to make sure you're eating meat, because if you do not, you will waste away and die. This was the problem the pastor had when he was writing to the Hebrews. The problem for the Hebrews was that they had grown dull of hearing and were not yet ready to get to the meaty stuff (Heb. 5:11-14). The pastor wanted to talk to them about Melchizedek but they were in no space to pronounce his name, let alone understand his significance. In chapter one we thought a little bit about our positional holiness. We discussed how our position in Christ leads to how we are to live. Now we will think about what it means to grow up into our status. As Christians we want to grow in holiness. But only the right fuel will give us the growth that we want and need. I hope I have already proven that holiness is essential to the Christian life, and so you should be in a place of desiring that growth.

Different pastors and preachers have different approaches when it comes to urging congregations in holiness. My favourite kind of sermons used to be the kind that hit you over the head with a stick and left you on the floor in floods of tears. I think we have all heard the hammer style sermon where the preacher wacks us over the head and yells at us in order to stop us from sinning. You end up leaving the building in floods of tears, guilty of your ungodly life, and energized to live a new and righteous life. But if you're anything like me you'll notice that the buzz dies off half way through the week. You start off really well on Monday, you're conscious of the message, it's fresh in your mind, and you want to beat that pestering sin. By the time Tuesday comes around you're still up for the fight, but you're a little less enthusiastic than you had been the day before. By this stage you're starting to fear for the worst. When Wednesday comes it's gone completely, or if you're a little holier than me you might make it to Thursday. Whatever day it is for you you'll notice that the hammer style sermon usually dies off and produces no lasting fruit in your life. I'm not saying it can't, because it can, and I've seen the Lord use them. While this style of preaching and motivation for holiness has some short term benefit I'm convinced that it isn't sufficient fuel for real lasting change in the Christian life. It's kind of like a bodybuilder drinking protein shakes instead of going to the effort of cooking steak. It's ok, but it probably won't be great in the long run. Hammer driven sermons are also in stark contrast to the Bible's pattern. The reason that it doesn't work is multi-faceted, but let me give you one big reason. One day, a lawyer came up to Jesus and asked him this question, "Teacher, which is the greatest commandment in the Law?" That's a pretty good question because there were roughly 613 different laws in the Old Testament. Jesus responded to the lawyer with wonderful precision, "You shall love the Lord your God with all your heart and with all your soul and with all your mind. This is the great and first commandment. The second is like it: You shall love your neighbour as yourself. On these two commandments depend all the Law and the Prophets" (Matt. 22:34-40). Now do you notice something about the first commandment? The foremost command for the Christian is to love the Lord our God with all our *heart*, soul and mind. This means that only an obedience that springs from the heart is true obedience. And this is the ultimate problem with the kind of preaching I mentioned before. Fear driven exhortations do not, and cannot produce a heartfelt obedience to the commands of God. They only create a hypocritical performance where the Christian ends up seeing God as a hard task-master. We end up acting like Pharaoh who let God's people go against his will. This is not true holiness.

THE PROBLEM

A call to holiness that's anchored in fear driven motivations cannot bring lasting change in the Christian's life. Remember that true holiness must flow from the heart, as well as from the head and the soul. The reason then that fear driven commands don't work is because there's a huge problem humanity faces – our hearts love to sin. The Bible says we love the darkness because our works are evil (Jn. 3:19). It's our evil desires that give birth to sin (Jam. 1:14-15).

43

So Aristotle is profoundly unhelpful: you can't "become holy by doing holy things". It won't work because our hearts naturally love sin more than they love holiness. This is one of the greatest problems that's presented in the Bible. God's problem with his people was always that they had hard hearts that went after other gods. The tablets of stone was always a reflection of their stony hearts. The people of God could not obey God's law because their hearts were hard. The good news of the new covenant is that God promises to remove the heart of stone and put in it a heart of flesh. But while the Christian has a new nature and a new heart, he is still at war with sin each day and so he still succumbs to its power. And the reason why God's people sin remains the same. We sin because we love to sin, it comes from our desires. This Bible reality has profound implications for the Christian life. It changes the way we do everything, and even the way we deal with sin such as pornography. The solution in the past was to try and provide accountability, to take away any ability for the person to fall into sexual sin. And there are definitely some benefits for doing some of those things! But I wonder if you have noticed the problem with it? While we may stop a man looking at pornography by putting covenant eyes on his computer, and giving him accountability partners, we cannot deal with his heart. We have only dealt with the surface level problem. We've stopped the fruit, but haven't healed the root – his love and desire to sin. If we stop there and only put internet blockers on his phone we will stop the ability to look at pornography on the phone, but nothing more. The individuals heart has still not changed, and let's face it, in our technological age, there are thousands of ways to bypass that problem anyway. What we need is a much more powerful solution than setting up covenant eyes on our computer. Please don't mishear me, I think it's a great tool, and I'm an advocate for it. I just don't think we can stop there and think we will be ok. Something deeper needs to happen to the Christian is what I'm saying. We need to stop not only the fruit of sin, but get to the root of the problem - which is the love of sin.

THE SOLUTION

So what is the solution to our greatest problem? It sounds like there can't be a solution doesn't it? If the problem is our heart, then how on earth can we fix that… it's just not possible. I suggest that there are three solutions to our great problem. The three means by which we can have lasting growth in godliness are: the gospel, faith, and the Spirit of God.

THE GOSPEL

So if true holiness is a holiness of the heart as well as the mind and the soul, how can we grow in it? What is necessary for us to move on in the Christian life? A real and lasting holiness cannot be forced by fear, but only won by considering God's unconditional love and goodness towards us. This is the chief means God uses to grow his people in holiness. The Bible's pattern is the same from Genesis to Revelation. What God uses to bring us from a love of sin to a love of holiness is a reminder that he *already* loves us, and that our sins are already freely blotted out by Christ. The Bible tells us that God loved us while we were yet sinners (Rom. 5:8). It has always been this way from the beginning. When God gave the Israelites the Ten Commandments on Mount Sinai he first told them that they were already his new and redeemed people (Ex. 20:1-2). The Ten Commandments were never a new way for God's people to win favour with him, and merit eternal life. God was telling the Israelites how to live in his place, under his rule, as the already redeemed people of God. In the New Testament this pattern becomes even more apparent, as God reminds his people that they have been cleansed of sin through the death and resurrection of Jesus Christ. After reminding us of our new identity in Christ we are then urged to live a new and holy life. It is the grace of God that teaches us to say no to ungodliness (Tit. 2:11-12). It is God's kindness that leads us to repentance (Rom. 2:4). We offer up our bodies as living sacrifices in light of the mercies of God (Rom. 12:1-2). Over and over again, the New Testament authors urge us on to new life in light of what Jesus has already done. What Christ has done always comes before how we are to live. The cross of Christ is the very power to live a holy life. John Owen said that "Holiness is the writing of the gospel on our hearts". Without a clear grasp of the gospel we will never truly overcome sin and love holiness.

It is only when we grasp the love of God towards us in Christ that we have a new heart and desire to live for him. I am no longer a slave to sin, because I no longer love the sin that I once did. I have now begun to love the Lord Jesus which will be the only power that will enable me to live a new life to the glory of God. When we realise how much Jesus freely loves us, our hearts are then full of love to serve and live for him. We see this in action in Luke's gospel when a woman runs up to Jesus to clean his feet with her hair. Jesus explaining her actions says, "She loved much because she had been forgiven much." The woman was only able to love because she knew how much she had been forgiven. When we look to the cross we see a

God who loved us while we were sinners and rebels. We were the ones who put Jesus on the cross. Martin Luther would say that we always carry about in our pockets his nails. Winslow said that, "so completely was Jesus bent upon saving sinners by the sacrifice of himself, he created the tree upon which he was to die, and nurtured from infancy the men who were to nail him to the cross." That's staggering love, and it was for you and me. But it's not just reflecting on Jesus' love for us in the past, but reflecting on his love for us now. Jesus is the same yesterday, today, and forever (Heb. 13:8). The same burning heart that we see in Jesus as he's walking to the cross to win us back to God is the same burning heart he has for us now in heaven. We are told in the book of Hebrews that we don't have a high priest who is unable to sympathise with our weaknesses, but one who was tempted in every way that we have been, yet without sin (Heb. 4:15). The word 'sympathise' doesn't do the verse justice, it more has the idea of 'bowels being moved with complete compassion'. Jesus as the glorified God-man standing in glory still has compassion for us as we struggle here on earth. The surprising thing about that passage is that Jesus is compassionate towards us even while we sin. Thomas Goodwin once said, "your sin moves Christ more to pity than to anger." That is a truly wonderful thought. To think that when I sin Jesus is moved with pity towards me and desires greatly to slay not me, but the sin that's weighing me down. Most of us don't think about Jesus in this way, I certainly never did until I stumbled upon the works of the Puritans. They have an amazing ability to draw your heart out to the Christ who's heart moves for us. The gospel is central for our growth in holiness. When we think of what Jesus has done for us on the cross, and as we reflect on who Jesus is towards us now, we can't help but love him and submit to him in return. Who wouldn't want to submit to a king like that? A king who with his first words to the men who abandoned him and left him for dead were, "Go to my brothers". Brother and sister, let the gospel sink deep into your mind and heart, for it is only there that you will find the strength to holiness.

FAITH

The second aspect that enables us to live a holy life is faith. I have often heard it said that we are justified by faith and then sanctified by works. Faith is the instrument that God uses to get us into the kingdom by the means of Christ's sacrificial death, but then works is the way we achieve growth. Consider for a moment the previous chapter, and we will see very quickly how this cannot be the case. The faith that justifies us is the same faith that sanctifies us. This is all grounded in our union with Christ. When we receive Christ by faith we receive all of him, including sanctification, because Christ is our sanctification, as well as our justification (1 Cor. 1:3). In his letter to the Galatians, Paul says that he lives the Christian life by *faith* in the Son of God (Gal. 2:20). Paul is not talking about justification here because being justified isn't the life we live. Rather, Paul is talking about how he moves on in the Christian life. I used to believe that faith in Christ gets us into the kingdom, and then we move on to new and better things. I believed that faith was purely the entry point to salvation. But there is no moving onto anything, because there's nothing better to move on to. Faith in the Son of God is what gets us into the kingdom, and faith in the Son of God is what keeps us in the kingdom. Faith in who Christ is and what he has done for us. Now justification and sanctification are not the same thing, we absolutely want to avoid that conclusion at all costs. But we do need to uphold the fact that justification and sanctification are ours by faith in Christ.

Faith also enables us to walk in holiness because it is by faith that we trust the work of Christ. We believe along with Paul that through Christ we are dead to sin and alive to God (Rom. 6:2-3), that we can live by the Spirit (Gal. 5:25), and that for freedom Christ has set us free (Gal. 5:1). If we try and live by works instead of faith we are doomed to fail because faith takes hold of the promises of God towards us in Christ. Trying to white-knuckle it and force yourself to be more holy just won't work because of the nature of faith and grace. Saint Augustine said, "God commands what he wills and then gives what he commands." Augustine is saying that God's commands come from his own will, but then Augustine acknowledges that unless God helps us we will not be able to do what he has asked of us. God is the one who will give us the ability to walk in newness of life and that gift is given by grace through faith. It has always been the case that God's people grow in holiness through faith and by the Spirit. In Galatians 3 Paul says, "Let me ask you only this: Did you receive the Spirit by works of the law or by hearing with faith? Are you so foolish? Having begun by the Spirit are you now being perfected by the flesh... Does he who supplies the Spirit to you and works miracles among you do so by works of the law or by hearing with faith?" (Gal. 3:2-5). It you follow Paul's logic it becomes clear what he is saying. The Galatians received the Spirit, and therefore salvation, by faith, and they are only going to be perfected by that same faith. How could it be that God would have us begin by faith and then finish by works/the flesh?

THE HOLY SPIRIT

The third and final way Christians are able to grow in holiness is by the Holy Spirit. It doesn't matter how much we try and work at holiness, if the Spirit isn't at work in our lives there is absolutely no way we will be able to grow in sanctification. The Spirit is the one who made us born again to a living hope (Jn. 3:7-8). He is the one who brought new life into us and gave us new natures. It is also the Holy Spirit who puts our sin to death (Rom. 8:13). There is a famous book by John Owen titled, 'the mortification of sin', and in this book Owen argues that we can only put sin to death and grow in holiness when the Spirit is at work in our lives. Owen talks about the Roman Catholic church and how many of their members look to things like prayer, fasting, and meditation as the fountain, rather than the stream. What is he saying? Owen says that the Christian can only live virtuously by the Spirit and faith. Prayer, fasting and meditation springs from the work of the Spirit, rather than the other way round. The Spirit is the one who puts our sin to death, and he is the one who enables us to put on good works, after all they are called the fruit of the Spirit (Gal. 5:21). Without the Spirit working in our lives we will never be able to put sin to death or live to the glory of God.

John Owen then asks a logical question, "If this is the work of the Spirit alone, how can I possibly be exhorted to the work? If only the Spirit of God can do it, why don't we leave it all to him?" It's a good question isn't it? If this is the work of the Spirit then why bother trying at all... why don't we just sit around passively and wait for him to kill our sin? First, Owen shows us that the work that's done in us is really the work of God. God is the one who works in us according to his own good pleasure (Phil. 2:13), He works all our works in us (Isa. 26:12), and it is the work of faith with power (2 Thess. 1:11, Col. 2:12). Secondly, the Spirit does all of these things, but does them with us. "The Spirit works in us and with us, not against us, or without us." The Spirit works upon our understanding, our will, conscience and affections so that while he is really doing the work, we are truly doing the work as well. This is what theologians sometimes call compatibilism. The idea that God is completely sovereign and is at work, and humans are responsible and work as well. That's why Paul is able to tell us to work out our own salvation with fear and trembling, and then tell us that God is the one who's at work in us according to his good pleasure. Is God sovereign, or is man responsible? Yes. Both are true simultaneously. The Spirit does his work in us in such a way that we really desire to kill sin and put on the fruit of righteousness.

Another thing for us to consider is that Jesus Christ lived his entire life in complete dependence on the Spirit of God. After Jesus was dunked in the water during his baptism, the Spirit of God came down like a dove and rested on him. It was only as the Spirit anointed Messiah that Jesus lived his sinless life. A lot of theologians discuss the impeccability of Christ. Was he, or was he not able to sin given that he is God, and God cannot sin? Of course, the answer to that question is no, Jesus could not have sinned because Jesus is God. But it's a different question to ask, "Why didn't Jesus sin?" Why Jesus *couldn't* sin and why Jesus *didn't* sin are two different questions. Jesus couldn't have sinned because he is truly God, and God cannot be tempted with evil. But Jesus didn't sin because he relied upon the Holy Spirit during his earthly ministry. Jesus needed the Spirit during his temptation in the wilderness (Matt. 4:1); he needed the Spirit to cast out demons (Matt. 12:28); and he needed the Spirit to enable him to offer himself without spot to God as an atoning sacrifice for our sins (Heb. 9:14). If Jesus lived his entire life in complete dependence upon the Holy Spirit, what makes us think it would be different for us? If Jesus needed to rely on the Spirit during his earthly ministry, then we can be sure that we will need to rely upon him as well. After all the Scriptures tell us to, "walk by the Spirit and thereby not gratify the desires of the flesh" (Gal. 5:16). "If we live by the Spirit then let us also keep in step with the Spirit" (Gal. 5:25).

So, back to the original question at the beginning of the chapter: how do we grow in holiness? Ultimately not by feeling coerced into it, but by meditating on the gospel and what Jesus has done for us, living by faith, and walking by the power of the Spirit. It is only through these three means that God will enable you to be holy and live a transformed life. It is the gospel that produces faith, that produces love, from which come the good works that are pleasing in God's sight. Brother and sister – preach the gospel to yourself every day! Never stop meditating on what God has done for you in Christ. It will change your life.

REFLECTION QUESTIONS

- Why are fear driven exhortations fairly useless in producing lasting change in the Christian life?
- How might you implement a habit of daily reflection on the gospel more in your own life?
- What is it about the gospel that motivates you to holiness?
- How is the Holy Spirit at work to produce lasting change in your life?

CHAPTER FOUR

THE CHURCH AND HOLINESS

I wonder what comes to your mind when you think of the church? Maybe you think of an old gothic building with uncomfortable seats, filled with bells and smells? Perhaps you think of a charity organisation that helps feed the poor? For a lot of Christians, the church is that annoying thing on the side that we should probably 'do'. It's a bit of a pain, and I'd rather spend my Sunday sitting at home listening to super convicting Paul Washer sermons. That's kind of church anyway isn't it? The church isn't a building, it's people, therefore me and my Bible at home is me doing church, right? Wrong! Sitting at home on a Sunday, Bible in hand, watching Paul Washer sermons is not even close to being church. In fact, if you think that's church you haven't been listening to Washer very clearly in the first place! Church is the gathering together of God's people, not you in a room, and certainly not brick and timber. The church can't possibly be a building because writing to the Romans Paul says, "Greet the church that is in their house" (Rom. 16:5). Paul's talking about a group of people, not a building inside of a house. The church has been established by the Lord Jesus Christ and it is therefore a divine entity (Matt. 16:18-19). The church is also described in the Bible as the temple of God (1 Cor. 3:16), the body (1 Cor. 12), the bride (Eph. 5:25-27), and a holy nation (1 Pet. 2:9).

DO I NEED TO GO TO CHURCH?

People have thought about the church in two ways in the past. There's the universal church, which consists of every chosen believer from the beginning of time, until the last day when Jesus returns to consummate the new heavens and the new earth. There is also the local church, which consists of the visible expression of the universal church. Because of their theology of the universal church, some Christians think that they can get away with not bothering to meet in a local church. They might say something like this, "who cares about the local church? It's the universal church that I need to be a part of". I wonder if that's the way that you think about church? Maybe you've come to terms with the fact that church is good and beneficial for those who need it. But you're not really convinced that *you* need to turn up. At least, not every week? Isn't my level of attendance in church my own personal and private choice? It's a little cultish to check up on me isn't it? However you want to ask yourself this question, one thing is clear – your answer *must* be governed by God's word! The God who created us, rescued us, and set us apart has also called us to offer up our entire lives as living sacrifices to him (Rom. 12:1). God cares about what we do every day, including the Lord's Day, when the people of God have historically gathered. What we need to recognise is that the church is not personal, but corporate and congregational by definition. It's not a matter of personal preference. The local church *is* made up of individual Christians... *but* we've been joined together to make one body (1 Cor. 12:12, 27). This is why it makes no sense to have lone ranger Christians. To be in Christ and not connected to his body is a massive contradiction in terms.

Another reason people can be put off by church is because it has been used as a form of legalism in the past, and we definitely need to guard against that! Church attendance has definitely been used as a legalistic tool. We need to remember that we've been made right with God through faith in Jesus, not by our good works or church attendance (Eph. 2:8-9). However, salvation through faith in Christ always produces good works and obedience (Jam. 2:14-26). God's grace to us isn't grounds for us to disobey, but the very power to enable us to obey his loving commands (Tit. 2:11-12). This includes the command to not forsake meeting together corporately;

Let us not give up meeting together as some are in the habit of doing, but let us encourage one another… all the more as you see the day approaching (Heb. 10:25).

It's also worth considering that the Lord Jesus Christ himself was in the habit of meeting with God's people;

He went to Nazareth, where he had been brought up, and on the Sabbath day he went into the synagogue as was his custom (Lk. 4:16).

This doesn't mean that there won't be good reasons for being absent at church. There are a whole host of good and godly reasons to not be at church on a Sunday (illness, induced labour, annual leave and so on). That's church life in a fallen world! But I'm convinced that we are more willing to make excuses than not to. And it's to our detriment! It's the church where we experience the presence of God through the preaching of his word. It's the church where we encourage one another with songs, and build one another up in the most holy faith. Opting out of church doesn't just affect you! It affects the whole body of Christ to whom you belong. It affects the believers who seek mutual encouragement by your singing (Col. 3:16), and who look to be stirred up in love and good works (Heb. 10:24). It affects new Christians who would conclude from your example that Christian fellowship is insignificant, and that the word of God is a 'sometimes' food. It affects your non-Christian friends who see that Jesus and his people play second fiddle to your lifestyle hobbies. It affects your leaders who watch over your soul and seek your growth in the faith (Heb. 13:17). Your brothers and sisters need you (1 Cor. 12:20-21). God has gifted you in a way he hasn't gifted me, and vice versa! We need each other. A low attendance reveals a low understanding of the beauty of the local church. Church is not supposed to be an optional extra to my life, nor a perk of the faith I can fall back to. Every saved person has been saved out of the world and into the people of God. That's why the local church isn't a building, but the spiritual family that's been adopted into Christ. Under the headship of our Lord and Saviour we serve one another, love one another, honour one another above ourselves, contribute to one another's needs, rejoice and weep with one another, and live in harmony with one another (Rom. 12:3-16). How wonderful is that! It's not something you can do in isolation. You can't serve, and experience service when it's you in a room with a Bible.

HOLINESS AND THE MEANS OF GRACE

So what does any of this have to do with holiness? Why are we all of a sudden thinking about the church? The church is the place where we both put holiness on display, and receive the means of grace that enable us to be holy. In the last chapter we thought about the three means God uses to make us holy; the gospel, faith, and the Holy Spirit. Think about what happens when we gather together for a moment. The church is the place where the gospel is proclaimed, faith is renewed, and the Holy Spirit is at work. Because of this, church is vital for holiness. Something significant happens when the people of God gather on the Lord's Day to receive the means of grace. The preaching of the word and the administration of the sacraments are no small thing in the life of the believer. God has always worked powerfully by his word. Paul tells us that the Scriptures are able to make us wise for salvation, and profitable to equip us for every good work (2 Tim. 3:15-17). Jesus tells us that the word of God sanctifies us (Jn. 17:17). A church service is a conversation between God and man. We hear God speak to us his promises and commands, and we respond to God in singing and prayer. We're also that that the Scriptures were read, explained and unpacked (Neh. 8:8). This is the pattern in the Old Testament, it's commanded by Paul in the New Testament, and has been practised throughout church history. God works through his word and by his Spirit. You will become more holy when you hear Gods word, because God sanctifies his people through it. And then there are the two sacraments (Baptism and the Lord's

Supper). They are also used by God in our lives. They are glorious pictures of the gospel, and they are a means through which God extends his grace to us. That's because Baptism and the Lord's Supper are strongly linked to union with Christ as Romans 6 and 1 Corinthians 10 makes clear. When we take the cup and break bread together we are participating in the blood and body of Christ. Jesus says, "He who eats my flesh and drinks my blood has life." Of course we know Jesus isn't speaking literally, but figurately during this discourse, but there is a sense in which we experience spiritual blessings when we partake of the Lord's Supper together as God's people. As we receive the sacrament we are united to Christ by the power of the Spirit. Just as we have already been clothed with Christ, so the Scriptures tell us to put on Christ in a progressive sense. We are already united to Christ by the Spirit, and we are also to grow up in our union with Christ. God uses the means of grace to grow us up in our union with Jesus Christ. So can you grow in holiness without gathering with God's people? Maybe… but probably not. For one, can you be holy while disobeying God's clear word to gather with his people? And is holiness possible without the corporate means of grace? Again I say the same thing, probably not. The means of grace are *the* way that God works in his people. To desire holiness, and to avoid gathering with God's people are two separate things. You cannot desire to be holy and ignore God's clear command to gather with his people. And you cannot be holy without being in the space where God works through his word by the power of his Holy Spirit. Church life and holiness are inseparable.

HOLINESS ON DISPLAY

We receive holiness through the means of God's grace in church. And the church is also the place where holiness is put on display. If holiness is connected with being conformed to Christ and submitting to his will, then we must take the instruction of God's word seriously. Commands like, "Love one another as I have loved you" (Jn. 13:34), "Love one another with a brotherly affection. Outdo one another in showing honour. Do not be slothful in zeal, be fervent in spirit, serve the Lord. Rejoice in hope… contribute to the needs of the saints and seek to show hospitality." (Rom. 12:9-13). I'm not really sure how a Christian is able to obey God's word here if we've decided that church is 'me and my Bible at home'. I'm not sure what it means to grow in holiness without being among God's people. What does it look like to grow in love for others, to love people with a familial love, to outdo one another in showing honour, to show hospitality by getting people round for dinner, if we don't gather with anyone? I'm not sure how it's possible to grow in holiness in these ways by forsaking the gathering together of God's people. Clearly the way that we grow in holiness is by learning to bear with one another in love. Think for a moment about what it means to be Christ-like. Jesus is unbelievably patient and forgiving towards us. Every single day he forgives and bears with us. Becoming like Christ involves growing in patience, love, and forgiveness towards others. These are really hard things to do, but unless we're gathered with God's people we'll never be able to grow in them. Gathering together is vitally important when it comes to holiness. Holiness is put on display when we forgive the person who has wronged us. If you are anything like me you will have noticed that forgiveness is extremely difficult! What better way to grow in Christ-like forgiveness that being among a group of sinful people who you offend, and they offend you? Holiness is also put on display when we invite the weaker members of our church to our houses for lunch. It shouldn't be the case that the only people that gather around our table are the people who have shoes to take off at the front door. Holiness is put on display when we put our music preferences aside and rejoice in the fact that 'old Betty' over there is banging out an old hymn to the glory of God! Laying our preferences to one side is in stark contrast to a world where people do what they want. Our 'otherness' is displayed in *being* the church.

The people of God then, are a collective holy people. We embrace a holy worship. This means that the people of God worship God according to Scripture alone, not according to our own worldly wisdom. If God left worship up to us, we would be joining the Israelites in building a golden calf. But worship is holy and it's always according to God's revelation. God tells us how we are to worship him. That is holy. The people of God also proclaim a holy message. It is the gospel that we proclaim. It's no good spending our time proclaiming anything else, the world can do that better than we can! We have the everlasting gospel and it is so different to anything that the world can preach. The people of God also display a holy unity. The people of God are gathered from every tongue, nation and tribe, and there is nothing like it anywhere. There is nothing on earth like the unity which comes through Jesus Christ and his cross. He brings people together who wouldn't normally gather together. And so as we gather under the means of grace and display our distinct 'otherness' we can't help but be shaped by it. The church then is vital for holiness.

REFLECTION QUESTIONS

- What is the church?
- Why do we need the church?
- How have you been committed to gathering together with God's people?
- How do church and holiness relate to each other?
- How might the Lord use holiness in the life of the church?

CHAPTER FIVE

THE PRACTISE OF HOLINESS

I am an absolute stickler for keeping the time. I am convinced that the height of gospel-shaped living is turning up on time, or being five hours early. My wife, on the other hand is the complete opposite to me. She is way more relaxed, and will happily finish getting ready one minute before we need to be at a friend's house – who lives an hour away! I love my wife, and I love that we are different because it gives us opportunities to love and serve one another when the inclination is to blow up in anger. But I'm being serious... I couldn't feel better about myself than when I get the chance to explain to people that I love being punctual, I mean, I'm doing it right now! But it's time for me to get off my high horse and ask this important question: What does holiness look like in practise? Is it really the case that the climax of gospel-shaped living is getting to a friend's house early? Well, there's a danger in writing a chapter on the specific practise of holiness. The danger of writing a chapter on the practise of holiness is that it can be too ambiguous on the one hand, or too black and white on the other. But we must look at this together. Having considering *how* to be holy, we will see *what* holiness looks like on the ground.

The first thing to consider is the relationship between holiness as *otherness*, and holiness as *ethical purity*. I have argued in previous chapters that holiness ultimately means being set apart. God is the ultimate set apart one, far above his creation, and when he saved us he set us apart as his own possession. So how can I suddenly start talking about holiness as though it means purity of life? Well, I still maintain that the Bible is fundamentally clear that holiness is first and foremost about being set apart from what is common. It is to be different from the rest of the world. The reason for this is because there are items in the Old

Testament that were considered holy, and it obviously wasn't talking about moral purity. For example, the ground that Moses was standing on near the burning bush was called holy ground. The ground obviously doesn't possess any special ethical purity any more than the chair I'm sitting on does. It was holy because God had set it apart for a special purpose. But there is a secondary way of talking about holiness. While holiness primarily means otherness, it can also mean purity of conduct as well. Peter says, "As obedient children. Do not be conformed to the passions of your former ignorance, but as he who called you is holy, you also be holy in all your conduct since it is written, 'You shall be holy for I am holy.'" (1 Pet. 1:14-16). Holiness certainly comes with it the idea of being morally pure. God calls us to be set apart in the way that we live our lives, and that looks like living in a particular way, with a particular conduct. But holiness is much more than rule keeping and ticking the right boxes. It's easy for us to think we are holy because we have stayed away from drugs, served the poor, and dressed modestly. Ticking the right boxes doesn't mean that God has captured your heart, as the religious leaders of Jesus' day proved. You can do all the box ticking in the world and still be far from pleasing in God's sight. In fact, there are a lot of 'good', and 'nice' people out there who are not Christians, and do kind and courteous things. Holiness also looks nothing like the form of traditional fundamentalism that we are used to seeing. A fundamentalist mentality that tries to advocate no alcohol, no smoking, and no dancing is certainly something… but it's not Biblical holiness. Where that fundamentalist approach to holiness came from, I have no idea, but we need to take that cat out the back and shoot it. I remember when I first became a Christian, and I thought the height of spirituality was the fact that I didn't watch Harry Potter and my other Christian friends did. It took me a long time to realise how ridiculous that was, and how unholy and proud my heart was about it! Holiness is much more than all of those small things. So what does holiness look like on a practical level?

CONFORMITY TO CHRIST

First and foremost, holiness looks like conformity to
Jesus Christ. Something big and cosmically
significant happened when the Son of God took on
flesh and dwelt among us. In the Lord Jesus Christ we
see a picture of what true humanity should have been.
Of course, Jesus isn't only our example. If Jesus was
only our example, and not our substitute, we would be
helpless and hopeless. Jesus is firstly the
substitutionary sacrificial Lamb who died in our place
and bore God's wrath for us. But we don't want to
pendulum swing so far away to the side of suggesting
that Jesus is not our example in any kind of way. The
first letter of Peter uses Jesus as our example on
numerous occasions. Do you want to know what it
looks like to suffer in a holy manner when you're
facing persecution? "For to this you have been called,
because Christ also suffered for you leaving you an
example, so that you might follow in his steps. He
committed no sin, neither was deceit found in his
mouth. When he was reviled he did not revile in

return, when he suffered he did not threaten, but continued entrusting himself to the one who judges justly." (1 Pet. 2:21-23). Do you want to know what it looks like to live a life of humility when you're tempted to serve your own needs? "Have this mind among yourselves which is yours in Christ Jesus, who though he was in the form of God, did not count equality with God a thing to be grasped, but emptied himself, by taking the form of a servant, being born in the likeness of men. And being found in human form he humbled himself to death, even death on a cross." (Phil. 2:5-8). Jesus is constantly held out to us in the New Testament as the perfect human. Holiness ultimately looks like Christ-likeness. Jesus is the one who has restored the image of God in us by his death and resurrection. We have been born again through the resurrection of Jesus from the dead (1 Pet. 1:3). Our new nature is a result of the resurrection of Jesus! And the goal of our redemption is to be conformed to the image of Jesus (Rom. 8:29). If I want to look like anyone, I want to look like Jesus! He is the perfect human, and he has lived like no one else on earth has lived. Jesus is a picture of who Adam should have been. Adam was created in the beginning to have close fellowship with God and enjoy communion with him. Instead, Adam chose sin and plunged us all into sin and ruin. And so we see in Jesus what it looks like to be truly human. Do you want to be holy? Then look to Jesus! He is our example for love (Jn. 13:34), our example in humility (Phil. 2:5-8), our example in our obedience to God (Jn. 6:38), our example for facing temptation (Heb. 4:15), and our example for endurance through suffering (1 Pet. 4:1-2). Jesus was gentle, pure, merciful, obedient, truthful, joyful, steadfast, submissive, and loved God and his neighbour perfectly. If you want to know what it means to be holy look to Jesus Christ. Paul exclaims that we'll be transformed into Christ's likeness when we behold him and his glory (2 Cor. 3:18). Get into the habit of meditating on the person of Jesus and consider how altogether lovely and wonderful he is. When I was a bodybuilder, I wanted nothing more than to look like Arnie. Now that I'm a Christian I want nothing more than to look like Jesus!

PUTTING OFF AND PUTTING ON

Another category for us to think about when it comes to holiness is the idea of putting off sin, and putting on the fruit of the Spirit. In other words, holiness has negative and positive aspects to it. The Puritans would often call this 'mortification' and 'vivification.' What they are saying is that we are to kill sin (which is the negative action), and put on good deeds (which is the positive action). This concept can be seen most clearly in the book of Galatians. But before we turn there it is worth pointing out that there are plenty of virtue and vice lists in the Bible to help us out with this. If you want to know what sins to avoid, and what virtues to put on, have a read of some of these lists. One of the expansive vice lists is found in the book of Romans,

Impurity, homosexuality, unrighteousness, evil, covetousness, malice, envy, murder, strife, deceit, maliciousness, gossip, slander, hatred of God, disobedient to parents, foolish, faithless, heartless, ruthless (Rom. 1:24-31).

In the book of Romans, Paul has been building up an argument which he started in verses 14 and 15. He is under obligation to preach the gospel to the church at Rome. That's what he's all about, and that's why he is writing the letter to them – he wants to get the gospel to them! Paul then gives us three reasons why he wants to get the gospel to Rome. The first reason is because the gospel is God's power to save. *For* I am not ashamed of the gospel because it is the power of God for salvation (Rom. 1:16). The second reason is because the gospel upholds God's righteousness, and because God gives that righteousness to sinners through faith. *For* in the gospel the righteousness of God is revealed from faith for faith, as it is written, "the just shall live by faith" (Rom. 1:17). The final reason is because God's wrath is being poured out on the world and people need to be saved. *For* the wrath of God is being revealed from heaven against all ungodliness and unrighteousness of men (Rom. 1:18). Do you follow Paul's logic? He wants to get the gospel to the church at Rome because it saves sinners, it upholds God's righteousness, and because God is angry at the world. People need to flee to Christ before they perish. God is angry at the world because humanity is living in sin and depravity. And the list Paul gives at the end of the chapter are the kinds of sins that engulf our world. You want to avoid these sins because God's anger is coming against all those who indulge in them.

Just like the vice lists, there are a number of virtue lists that can be found throughout the New Testament. One such list can be found in the same book of Romans,

Let love be genuine. Abhor what is evil; hold fast to what is good. Love one another with a brotherly affection. Outdo one another in showing honour. Do not be slothful in zeal, be fervent in spirit, serve the Lord. Rejoice in hope, be patient in tribulation, be constant in prayer. Contribute to the needs of the saints and seek to show hospitality. (Rom. 12:9-13).

What is Paul getting at in this section of the letter? Well, Paul has just spent eleven chapters proclaiming the glorious gospel and the riches of God's grace. He then finishes chapter 11 by being swept away in praise and adoration. It is the gospel that Paul has proclaimed in the first eleven chapters which gives us the grounds for the way we are to live. That's why Paul begins this new section by saying, "I appeal to you therefore brothers, in light of the mercies of God, to present your bodies as a living sacrifice, holy and acceptable to God which is your spiritual worship." (Rom. 12:1). It is in light of the mercies of God, what God has done for us in Jesus Christ, that we are to live a new and transformed life. So the list that we find in verses 9-13 are a right response to the gospel. We have a Saviour that has loved us with a genuine love, who has hated evil, held fast to good, loved us with affection. Jesus has outdone us in showing honour, he was never slothful in zeal, but fervent in spirit and he served God. he rejoiced in hope, was patient in his tribulations, and was constant in prayer. Jesus contributed to our greatest need and shows us

hospitality in the greatest of all ways. Paul is calling
the church to live in light of the gospel.

The clearest place that we see the concept of
mortification and vivification is in the letter Paul
wrote to the Galatians. Paul has been building up a
case from the beginning that the law is useless when it
comes to inheriting the promises of God. The passage
is worth quoting in full,

*But I say walk by the Spirit and you will not gratify
the desires of the flesh. For the desires of the flesh are
against the Spirit, and the desires of the Spirit are
against the flesh, for they are opposed to each other...
Now the works of the flesh are evident: sexual
immorality, impurity, sensuality, idolatry, sorcery,
enmity, strife, jealousy, fits of anger, rivalries,
dissensions, divisions, envy, drunkenness, orgies, and
things like these. I warned you as I warned you before
that those who do such things will not inherit the
kingdom of God. but the fruit of the Spirit is love, joy,*

peace, patience, kindness, goodness, faithfulness, gentleness, self-control, against such things there is no law... if we live by the Spirit, let us also keep in step with the Spirit. (Gal. 5:16-25).

The point is obvious. Paul is saying, "Here's a list of sins that come from the flesh. These things are opposed to the Spirit and so put these things off. And here's a positive list, and these are the fruit of the Spirit. If you want to gratify the desires of the flesh, then ignore the Spirit's work. But if you want to put your flesh to death you need to walk in step with the Spirit and put on his fruit." There is a holy war that is going on inside every Christian. We have indwelling sin, and the Spirit. The Spirit is against the flesh and the flesh is against the Spirit. Growing in holiness then, is to put to death the sins that once entangled us, and to put on the virtues that come through the power of the Spirit.

HEAD HEART HANDS

A true holiness needs to include a renewing of the mind, a transformation of the heart, and a service towards others. I'm a heady and hearty kind of guy, and so I find serving other people practically to be a really difficult thing to do. I much prefer getting stuck into Christian books and growing in my understanding of who God is and who we are. I also love to read the Puritans and reflect on who Christ is towards sinners in order to "feel my heart strangely warmed". A renewing of the mind, and an engagement of the heart come a lot easier to me than practically loving people with my hands. But the mature Christian is someone who grows in their thoughts, loves, and deeds.

A holiness of the head is shaped by the word of God. God's word constantly shapes how we understand the world. We are born in sin, and we live in a culture that preaches a different narrative to the narrative God speaks. And so we constantly need to be washing ourselves in the word of God. Holiness looks like reading your Bible. I know that's a boring comment, and I have lamented at the simple, "Read you Bible and pray" sermon applications. But reading the Bible is a holy thing to do, because it is there that we meet with God, learn to love him, and are shaped by him. Paul exhorts the church at Rome to "not be conformed to this world, but to be transformed by the renewal of the mind, that by testing you might discern what is the will of God, what is good and acceptable and perfect." (Rom. 12:2) Holiness looks like renewing your mind and conforming yourself to God's ways. That ultimately happens as we engage with God's word and allow it to work its way into our heads.

A holiness of the heart is also shaped by God's word. It's not enough to be holy in our thinking, we need to be holy in our inner most being. When I encountered and embraced the Reformed position on the sovereignty of God I began to lap up all and every teaching on it. But I must confess that my heart was hardly changed by it – that's a problem! The Bible says we need to love God with our whole heart, as well as our mind. The heart is not a soppy word for the subjective feelings and tingles that we get. The heart is the epicentre of who we are. Our heart is what directs and guides us. "Keep the heart with all vigilance, for from it flows the springs of life (Prov. 4:23). The heart is what drives us and our affections. And holiness looks like working on our hearts. Our hearts are conformed to God's will in the same way our minds are; through the reading of God's word. Holiness looks like being driven and guided by God's word.

A holiness of the hands is also shaped by God's word. A head that's renewed, and a heart that's transformed *should* lead to a practical outworking of service. I say should, but so often it doesn't. Holiness looks like serving other people in practical ways. Do the members in my church lack anything? How can I be of service to them? Get down in the dirt, and practical.

OBEYING GOD'S WORD

Holiness looks like being conformed to the image of
Christ, as well as living a life of mortification and
vivification. But holiness also looks like being
obedient to the commands of God. This is probably
one of the most controversial points to make in the
chapter. With the rise of New Covenant theology,
many Christians are arguing that we don't need to
obey the law anymore because we are no longer under
the law. Instead, they argue that believers are under
the law of Christ. This is a deep and complex
discussion and I don't have time to go into the details
here, and for that I'm sorry! There are wiser and
smarter people than me who have had that discussion.
All I will say is that I see no Biblical reason to discard
the Old Testament commandments for a number of
reasons. First, they are used by Jesus, and the Apostles
as guide for how to live. When a rich young ruler asks
Jesus what he must do to inherit eternal life, Jesus
responds by giving him the second half of the law.
Likewise, Paul in Romans 13 lists a number of the

Ten Commandments as things we should be obeying. The second reason I wouldn't discard the law is because of the promise that we find in Jeremiah. God promises that the New Covenant will be better than the Old Covenant, because in the new God will write his law on our hearts. I'm not really sure what else that could be other than the law of Moses. How could it be the law of Christ, when Jeremiah had no concept of the law of Christ? It must mean Mosaic law.

Enough of that debate, and into the discussion of holiness by the commands of God. The Scriptures make it clear that we are called upon to obey God's commands. We can be confident that we have come to know God and share in his salvation when we obey him and keep his commandments (1 Jn. 2:3). Jesus said that if we love him we'll obey his commands (Jn. 14:23). One of the sure signs that we love the Lord Jesus is if we submit to him and obey what he says. But you might ask: What are the commands of Jesus?

Well, it's obvious isn't it? Open your Bible's and find all the places where the verses are packed full of red letters. Then read them, digest them, and obey them! Sorry, I'm being facetious. As Jesus is God, and the Bible is breathed out by God, every command on every page, in every book, in both Testaments, in the whole Bible is given by Jesus Christ. A great place to begin thinking about how to obey Jesus is to start opening the Bible. The commands of God from Genesis to Revelation are given by Father, Son and Spirit. The ultimate way to obey God is to love him with our heart, mind and soul, and to love our neighbour as ourselves. And if you want something a little more concrete than that, then the Ten Commandments is a pretty good summary of what it looks like to love God, and love our neighbour. Christians don't always agree on how to view the Ten Commandments, but it is a good summary of what it looks like to love God and neighbour. For Jesus and the Apostles, the Ten Commandments were a basic summary of God's ethical intentions. When a rich man asks Jesus about inheriting eternal life Jesus points him to the Ten Commandments (Mk. 10:19). God's law is much more than the Ten Commandments, but it's not less. Therefore, a holy life will be a life lived in obedience to God's commands.

So what does holiness look like practically? Holiness looks like Jesus Christ. Jesus is the true human who lived the perfect life that we should have lived. A good place to begin thinking about holiness is reading and beholding the Lord Jesus Christ. He is the one we are being conformed to. Holiness also looks like killing sin and putting on good deeds. There are tens of vice and virtue lists in the Bible that you can feast your heart on. I suggest going through the Bible and meditating on some of those lists, and pray, asking the Lord for growth. Holiness looks like renewed heads, enlarged hearts, and working hands. Finally, holiness looks like obeying the commands of God. To obey God's word is to obey God himself, and Jesus says, "if you love me, obey my commands."

REFLECTION QUESTIONS

- What is the danger of having a tidy list of holy rules?
- In what ways does Christ exemplify holiness?
- How have you been impacted by looking at the Lord Jesus this week?
- What do the terms, 'mortification' and 'vivification' mean?
- Is it reasonable for New Covenant Christians to obey the Ten Commandments?

CHAPTER SIX

LEADERS AND HOLINESS

Donald Trump becoming the President of the United States sent shock waves around the world. Nobody could quite believe it that Trump was sitting in that chair, with that authority. It is an enormous and privileged position to be the President of the United States. There have been some interesting characters in the White House during the years, but maybe none so interesting as President Donald Trump. He seems to have grabbed attention like no one else before, and it's not for good reasons. The reason that people are so mesmerised by Trump in office is because of his character, not just his credentials. Whatever you make of Donald Trump the President, Donald Trump the person, and Donald Trump the social media whiz are precarious characters to say the least. When Donald Trump says he will do something stupid like blow up

Iran, I am 50% sure that he might actually do it –
that's scary! One of the big reasons why people are so
distraught with Trump being the President of America
is because of his tarnished character. Character is
important when it comes to representing a country.
You don't want the sleazy, arrogant, racist,
condescending man representing what you know and
love.

YOU NEED TO CARE ABOUT THIS

The same is true of leadership in the church. A godly
character is of utmost importance for those who
shepherd God's flock. It's a disgrace to have someone
in office who slanders, bickers, sleeps around, and
lives in all kinds of immorality. The discussion on the
holiness of church leaders is important for every
member of the church, not just the pastor. If you are a
member of a local church, and you should be, you
need to care about this. You will be held accountable
on judgement day for the people that have shepherded

the church that you attend. When the Galatians began to listen to false teachers Paul held the whole church personally accountable for it (Gal. 1:6).

I remember studying at Bible college and feeling excited about pastoring a church one day. I couldn't wait to prepare sermons, deliver sermons, train young men, get stuck in to pastoral counselling, and provide for the needs of the sheep. And there's nothing wrong with any of that, because those are essentials! But looking back I realise that I had a distorted view of the ministry, at least I only saw half the picture. I was so absorbed with thinking about teaching, and reading, and preaching good sermons that I didn't particularly consider how important holiness is for the ministry. One of the big surprises for me was the day I turned to 1 Timothy and discovered that being 'apt to teach' was a small sentence among a giant passage advocating holiness. I had thought that the greatest marker of the minister was the ability to teach God's word faithfully. There is definitely a lot of truth to that statement, but it wasn't until I realised that 'teaching' was one line within a massive section on holy living that I began to swing the pendulum back a bit. The pastor needs to watch his doctrine *and* his life.

HOLINESS IS A CENTRAL QUALIFICATION

Let's take a look at the passage from 1 Timothy together. And remember again that this is crucially important, not just for pastors but also for members of a local church. You need to know what to look for in your elders and deacons. Now of course I'm not advocating for the ticket police, standing around, being scrupulous, and waiting for the leaders to trip up over the smallest of sins. I'm not saying that the pastor needs to be sinlessly perfect, nor even measure up to your own personal standards. What I am saying is that elders and deacons need to be above reproach, and display a mature level of the qualifications that we find in Paul's letter. Paul is writing his letter to young Timothy, and he is writing in order to show

Timothy how one ought to conduct themselves in the household of God (1 Tim. 3:15). This whole letter is a how-to guide for Timothy when it comes to church practise. In chapter one, Paul has warned Timothy about false teachers who have infiltrated the church in order to spread false doctrine, and then Paul ends up telling Timothy that he was shown mercy through the coming of the Lord Jesus Christ. In chapter two, Paul moves on to talking about how the church should pray for those in authority, in order for the gospel to spread in a peaceful land. Paul then finishes chapter two telling men and women how they ought to conduct themselves in the church of God.

Then in chapter three we have the qualifications for pastors, and it is worth quoting the passage in full so you can see how important the theme of holiness and godly character is;

The saying is trustworthy: If anyone aspires to the office of overseer he desires a noble task. Therefore, an overseer must be above reproach, the husband of one wife, soberminded, self-controlled, respectable, hospitable, able to teach, not a drunkard, not violent but gentle, not quarrelsome, not a lover of money. He must manage his own household well, with all dignity keeping his children submissive, for if someone does not know how to manage his own household, how will he care for God's church? He must not be a recent convert, or he may be puffed up with conceit and fall into the condemnation of the devil. Moreover, he must be well thought of by outsiders, so that he may not fall into disgrace, into a snare of the devil. (1 Tim. 3:1-7).

I hope you can see the emphasis of a godly character in this passage. Apt to teach while being crucially important, is only one small line within a whole section. The emphasis that Paul is making to Timothy is that an overseer is to be holy in character. A lot of churches go wrong in how they appoint elders and deacons in their churches. The qualifications for deacons comes right after the section on elders. One of the big differences between an elder and a deacon is that the elder is able to teach God's word. But the ability to teach God's word, and a holy life are unfortunately not always the traits churches look for in leaders. Age, success, and likeability can too often be the qualifications for people in leadership roles. But notice that age has little to do with becoming an elder and a deacon. In one sense, you would expect elders and deacons to be older in the faith, because with age usually comes gospel maturity as well. A godly character is usually built up over a long period of time. But older men should not automatically be qualified for leadership, and younger men should not automatically be disqualified. If a young man is displaying godly character and the ability to handle God's word faithfully there is nothing stopping him from becoming an elder in the church. If an old man is lacking in maturity, doesn't understand the Bible very well, and appears spiritually apathetic, he is not qualified to lead God's church. Business success is often another trait that churches look for in their leaders. But business success and pastoring a church are not the same thing. Being a good businessman does not qualify you to become a pastor, in fact it can distract from the work. Likeability does not qualify you to the leadership either. Someone can be well liked, and be ungodly in their private life. The interesting thing about the list that Paul gives Timothy is that these are virtues that we would want every follower of Jesus to have. Other than the ability to handle God's word, every Christian should be self-controlled, soberminded, hospitable, etc. That's why pastors are often called examples and leaders in Scripture. The pastor is someone who models a godly life to the church. Writing to the Hebrews, the author tells the church to imitate the faith and life of their leaders (Heb. 13:7). Being more like Christ is what every Christian is called to be, and the leaders of the church get to put that holy life on display for the sheep to catch on and imitate.

WHY IS HOLINESS ESSENTIAL FOR LEADERS?

Robert Murray M'Cheyne famously said that, "The greatest need of my people is my personal holiness." Holiness is a great need for God's people because holiness is a means through which God saves the sheep. Now before you begin picking up stones and chucking them at me, consider the words of Paul again in his letter to Timothy, "Keep a close watch on your *life* and doctrine. Persist in this, for so by doing you will save both yourself and your hearers." What's Paul saying? He's obviously not saying that pastors are the active agents in bringing people to salvation. It is the Lord God who brings people from death to life in Christ. But Christ has chosen to bring people from death to life through the means of his word and God's people. when the word of Christ, and the character of Christ are displayed in the local church, non-believers will be attracted and drawn to Jesus. This is why pastors must guard the truth, because it is by the truth that people are saved. This is why pastors must guard their lives, because by their lives people see the difference that Christ makes. The gospel of transformation looks more powerful when people can see that you are actually transformed. Living a life of licentiousness and sin drags the gospel, and the Lord Jesus through the mud. Just consider Roman Catholicism for a moment. The Roman Catholic church is a false church that preaches a false gospel. I'm not saying that they are a true church, because they are not. But the world is unable to truly discern the big difference between a Protestant evangelical church, and Roman Catholicism. Sure, there's less bells and smells, and fancy dresses, but the world is not a specialist in understanding the main differences. And so as the heinous sin that has swept through the Roman church has been unveiled, we get caught up in the mess as well. The abuse that has famously gone on in Roman Catholicism has hurt not just them, but us as well. Holiness matters because an unholy life has no salt or light. An unholy life makes it look like Jesus is unable to transform anyone. Holiness is therefore crucial in the life of church leaders for two reasons.

First, the sheep will look at the example of the pastor and follow along. Second, the world will look at the lives of the sheep, who are following the pastor, and will make a judgement call on what they see. Pastors, church members, your holiness matters, eternal souls are on the line!

I want to conclude this chapter with a quick note on what to do if you are in a local church with ungodly and unqualified elders. The first thing to do is pray. Don't be hasty and cause division. Instead pray that the Lord God would change the hearts of your elders and make them more like Christ. God is perfectly able to do something like that. And second, speak to the elders about it, but do it with gentleness and love. Don't rebuke an elder, but exhort them like you would a father (1 Tim. 5:1). Pray, speak gently, and if after a good while there is no change, I would definitely consider finding a local church with godly qualified elders. Unholy elders bring the gospel into disrepute.

REFLECTION QUESTIONS

- Who qualifies someone to be a leader in a local church?
- Why is a discussion on church leaders relevant to every member in the church?
- Why is it necessary for a church leader to be holy?
- How does doctrine and life have an effect on people's eternal destinations?

CHAPTER SEVEN

THE GOSPEL AND HOLINESS

There is a strange phenomenon that happens to bodybuilders. The bigger you get the smaller you feel. Before I entered the bodybuilding scene I was a skinny fat kid who couldn't care less about his body. I really didn't care. I was skinny, but with a small gut, and it didn't bother me at all. It was only when I began training, and getting into the bodybuilding scene that I began to care a lot about my body and what it looked like. The mirror would often play devilish tricks on me. It didn't matter how big I was getting, I always felt and looked small in the mirror. It would play on my mind all day, every day. It was a horrible head space to be in. All I wanted was to grow in size, and yet I felt like I was smaller than ever. Holiness can often feel like that. The more I desire growth, the less holy I feel.

Holiness is one of those topics that can get the best of us down. When we look at our own lives it is so easy to see the negatives and wonder whether we are even saved at all. If you are anything like me you probably look at your life and sometimes wonder whether the Spirit is truly at work. Hopefully those days are far and few between, but they do sometimes come along. The honest truth about holiness is that it is the long game in the Christian life. Holiness takes time, and it is often painful. Holiness often comes through mistakes, at least it has in my own life. But on the off chance that you notice some growth, it is super encouraging. When you notice a more gracious tone in your voice to someone who is disagreeing with you. When you notice that you are starting to hang out with the people at church who don't smell and look like you. When you notice new and holy affections for the Lord Jesus Christ, you begin to see some of the true joys of holiness. Holiness can be a massive joy, and it is certainly a joy when you are in the presence of someone who exemplifies holiness. I have met a couple of people like that in my life, and when you are in their presence you don't want them to leave. They seem to glow talking about Christ, they are gentle and gracious, they listen well and care for the needs of others. In other words, they look a lot like the Lord Jesus Christ. These are the kinds of people that you want to be around, and these are the kinds of people that you want to emulate.

But let's be honest… discouragements come around more than encouragements do. And there's a lot of reasons for that. One of those reasons is that as I have said before, growth in holiness can take a long time. We are not talking days, nor even months, but years and decades. And the other difficulty with holiness is that the more holy you become, the less holy you realise yourself to be. As you become more holy, more of your blind spots are removed and you realise just how bad you are. I remember one of my theology lecturers telling me that he didn't realise he had a problem with popularity until he gave up his position of being the Principal of a Bible college. The growth in holiness comes with it the deeper understanding of our own sin. That's why we need to get other Christians in our lives who are able to give encouragements when we need them. People who are able to see us over the space of years and decades, people who can see the change that Christ has brought into our lives. People are able to see the change that Jesus has wrought upon your life because they see you over long periods. They don't live in your head every day like you do! And so get good Christian brothers and sisters into your life who can let you know how you are going. Even spend some time asking them, "Hey, how do you think I am going in my walk with Christ? Do I appear more patient, gracious, kind, and forgiving that I did five years ago?" By the grace of God your Christian family will be able to tell you how they have seen you grow more into the likeness of Christ. It is also good to get into the habit of encouraging other Christians about their growth in the faith as well. A great way to stop worrying about yourself is to focus on loving other people.

THE GOSPEL

We've been talking about the importance of holiness. And it is super important! It is who God is and who he calls us to be. Holiness is what we are saved for, and without some growth in holiness we should be concerned about our spiritual health. But whatever you do, don't forget the gospel. If you spend too much time observing your own life you will be discouraged, and you will feel downcast. Being beat up all the time over the sin in your life is not a good place to stay. While we need to be in the habit of considering our lives and how we are living, we also need to remember why Christ came. Jesus died for sinners, and he continues to uphold sinners. The way to move in the way of Christ is to preach the work of Christ. Robert Murray M'Cheyne said, "Learn much of your own heart, and remember you've only seen a few yards of a pit that is unfathomable when you've begun. And yet for every one look at yourself, take ten looks at Christ. He is altogether lovely. Such infinite majesty and yet such meekness and grace, and all for sinners. Live much in the smiles of God and bask in his beams. How many millions of dazzling pearls are hidden in the deep recesses of the ocean. Likewise, unfathomable oceans of grace are in Christ for you, you will never come to the bottom of these depths." For every one look at yourself, take ten looks at Christ. There's not much more to say than that. Looking to Jesus Christ is the only way to feel comforted during times of great discouragement. I realise a book on holiness can do that to people. While you may feel like you've grown in understanding, you could be left feeling deflated by your lack of holiness. You may have a picture in your mind of a God who is wagging his finger at you with disappointment each day. He's pretty ticked off and you're not sure that he's going to want to take care of someone like you. Why would he listen to your prayers given your sin? John Owen once said that the greatest injury we can give to God is... Now I wonder how you would finish that sentence? The greatest injury we can give to God is sinning? Living in wickedness? No, the greatest injury you can give to God is not believing that he loves you. If you feel robbed of joy you need to be drawn to the cross again, to see the place where God loved you *while* you were a sinner. God set his love upon us while we hated him. "I sometimes think about the cross, and shut my eyes and try to see, the cruel nails, and crown of thorns, and Jesus crucified for me. But even could I see him die, I could but see a little part, of that great love which like a fire, is always burning in his heart." While we desire to live a holy life we must remember that we will not be perfect until Christ finally returns. On that day we will be perfect, and in that we can rejoice. Let's finish with the words of C. S. Lewis,

"No amount of falls will really undo us if we keep picking ourselves up each time. We shall of course be very muddy and tattered children by the time we reach home. But the bathrooms are all ready, the towels put out, and the clean clothes are in the cupboard. The only fatal thing is to lose one's temper and give up. It's when we notice the dirt that God's most present to us, it's a very sign of his presence."

REFLECTION QUESTIONS

- In what ways have you been encouraged, and discouraged in your personal holiness?
- What person in your life could you ask to see how you're going with personal holiness?
- How might you be able to encourage others this week in their growth?
- How is it possible that the more holy we become, the less holy we feel?
- How does looking to Christ take us out of despondency?

CONCLUSION

I have been discouraged by my lack of holiness more times than you could count. I greatly desire to live a more holy life, and I am completely frustrated by the sin that so easy entangles me. But holiness has become more enjoyable to me the more I have understood what it is and the means through which God accomplishes it. I hope you have come to a better understanding of holiness as this book draws to a close. Holiness is a vitally important aspect of the Christian life. Indeed, living a holy life is the goal of our redemption. The Bible makes it clear that we are saved in order to be holy and blameless in God's sight. The importance of holiness is seen in the fact that we serve a holy God. "Holy Holy Holy is the LORD God almighty, the earth is full of his glory." Our God is so holy that the angels have to cover their faces in his sight. A holy God should be nothing but terrifying to sinners like us. A holy God cannot stand in the presence of evil. But the wonderful truth of the gospel that we have come to know through God's word is that God has already set us apart as holy in his Son. Holiness is already something that we are because of what Jesus did that day on Calvary. God now calls us to live in light of who we are – the bride that has been united to Jesus Christ. As the bride of Christ, we are called to be holy, and empowered to be holy through the gospel, faith, and the Holy Spirit. We get to experience the power of these means when we gather together as the people of God under the godly leaders that he has provided. It is there that we also get to display our holiness in the way that we love and serve one another. Holiness looks like conformity to Jesus Christ, and obedience to his word. Holiness is central to the Christian life. Holiness is what we are called to be. Perfectly holy is what we will eventually be when Christ returns to consummate the new heavens and the new earth. On that day, evil will be no more, only a kingdom where righteousness dwells forever and ever.

NOTES

- J. I. Packer, *Rediscovering holiness: Know the fullness of life with God* (Ventura, CA: Regal, 2009)
- J. C. Ryle, *Holiness: Its nature, hindrances, difficulties, and roots* (Peabody, MA: Hendrikson, 2007)
- Stephen Charnock, *Existence and Attributes of God, in the works of Stephen Charnock* (1864; repr. Edinburgh: Banner of Truth, 2010)
- Edward Leigh, *Treatise of Divinity: Consisting of three books* (London: E. Griffin for William Lee, 1647)
- Martin Luther, *The freedom of a Christian* (Minneapolis, MN: Fortress Press, 2008)
- John Calvin, *Institutes of the Christian Religion,* ed. John T. McNeil, trans. Ford

Lewis Battles, Library of Christian classics, vols 20-21 (Philadelphia: Westminster, 1960)

- Marcus Johnson, *One with Christ* (Wheaton, IN: Crossway, 2013)
- Walter Marshall, *The gospel mystery of sanctification* (US: Lightening Source, 2001)
- Thomas Goodwin, *The heart of Christ* (Edinburgh: Banner of Truth, 2015)
- Saint Augustine, *Confessions*
- John Owen, *The mortification of sin* (Ross-shire: Christian Focus Publications, 2006)
- Kevin Deyoung, *The hole in our holiness* (Wheaton, IN: Crossway, 2012)
- Andrew Bonar, *The Life of Robert Murray M'Cheyne* (Edinburgh: Banner of Truth, 1990)
- C. S. Lewis, *Letter to Mary Neylan,* January 20, 1942

Printed in Poland
by Amazon Fulfillment
Poland Sp. z o.o., Wrocław